MY BOW-ARM METHOD

For

Viola

Based on Open Strings Exercises

Beginners
Volume I

©2013
By Rafael M. Ramirez, DMA
All Rights Reserved

My Bow-Arm Method for Viola
Based on Open Strings Exercises
Beginners. Volume I (First Edition)

All Rights Reserved ©2013

Credits
Author: Rafael M. Ramirez O., DMA
Editor: Maria A. Bermudez M.
Cover Designer: Norman Bermudez M.
Illustrator: Rafael M. Ramirez O., DMA
Digitalization of Illustrations: Norman Bermudez M.
Models: Armando Torrealba, and Gabriel J. Ramirez
Prepared for Publishing by: María A. Bermúdez M.

Introduction

MY VIOLA BOW-ARM METHOD establishes a logical sequence of exercises, giving the viola student and teacher a sequential lesson plan to address bow technique. Each exercise is targeted to achieve mastery of a specific technical element of bowing. Fun and engaging imagery is used for younger students. Exercises increase progressively in difficulty for advanced students to ensure proficiency in all elements of viola bow technique.

The most important objective of this method is to assist the viola player to prepare for an everyday practice session. The method will help to develop bow control.

TABLE OF CONTENTS

ELEMENTARY RUDIMENTS 06
    Parts of the Viola 06
    Parts of the Bow 07
    An Introduction to Music Theory 08
    The Pitches 08
    The Music Staff 08
    The Clef 08
    The Alto Clef (C-Clef) 09
    The Treble Clef (G-Clef) 09
    Names of the Spaces and the Lines of the Music Staff 09
    The Beat 10
    Note Duration 10
    Parts of the Note 11
    Rests 11
    Time Signatures 11
    The Repeat Bar 12
    Dynamics 12
    Rhythm 12
    Bow direction 13

EXERCISES FOR CHILDREN 14
    Knowing our friend the bow 15
    Holding the Bow 16
    The Spider 18
    The Rocket-bow 20
    The Clock 22
    The Rotunda 24
    The Bow Knight 26

The Jump of Mr. Frog	28
The Bow Train	30
My Bow Plane	32
BOW ARM EXERCISES	34
Single String Exercises	34
Two String Crossing Exercises	48

ELEMENTARY RUDIMENTS

It is important to know the basics before playing the viola. This chapter will help the student to understand the fundamental elements of the viola such as: parts of the viola, parts of the bow, basic music theory, and more.

Parts of the Viola

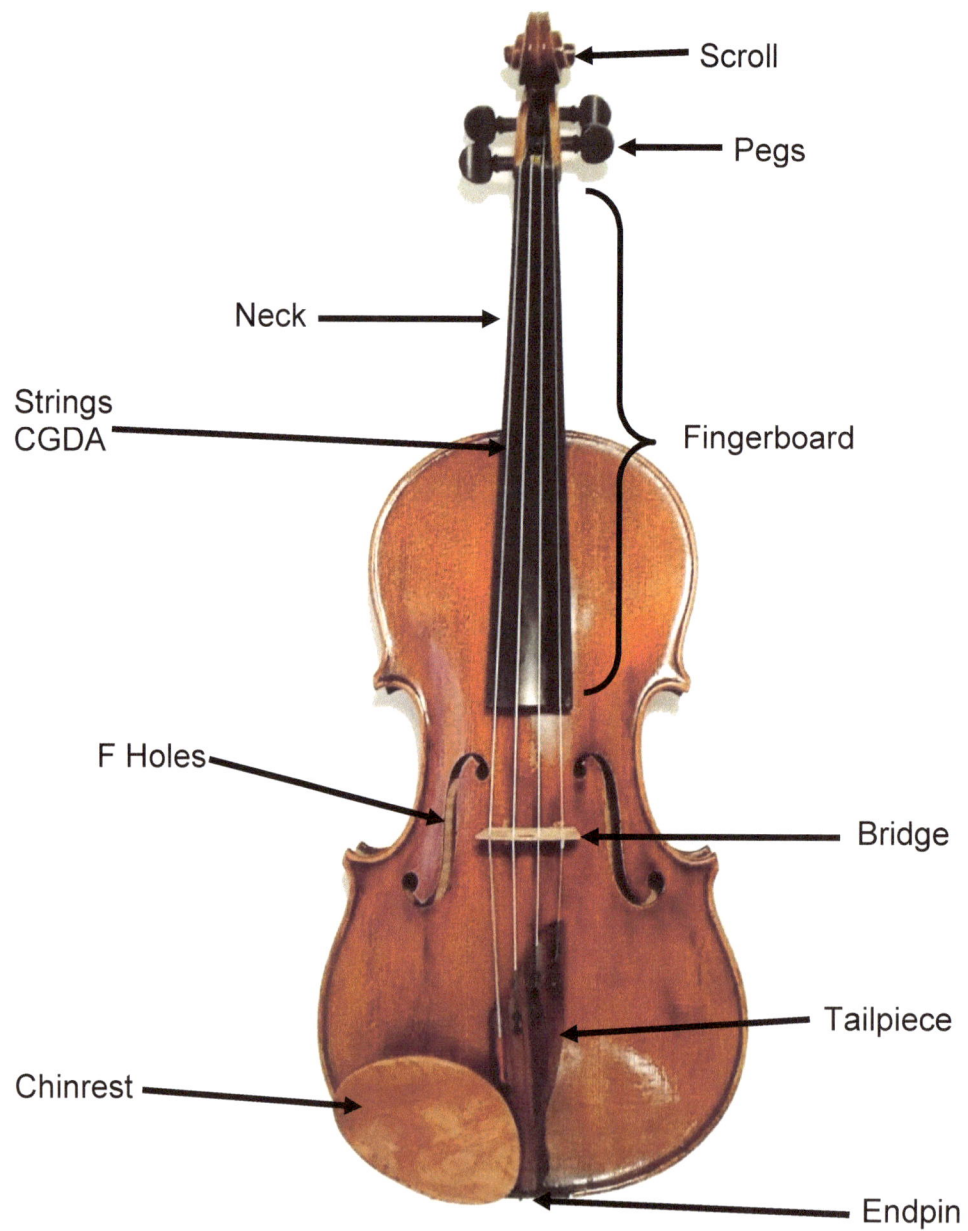

Parts of the Bow

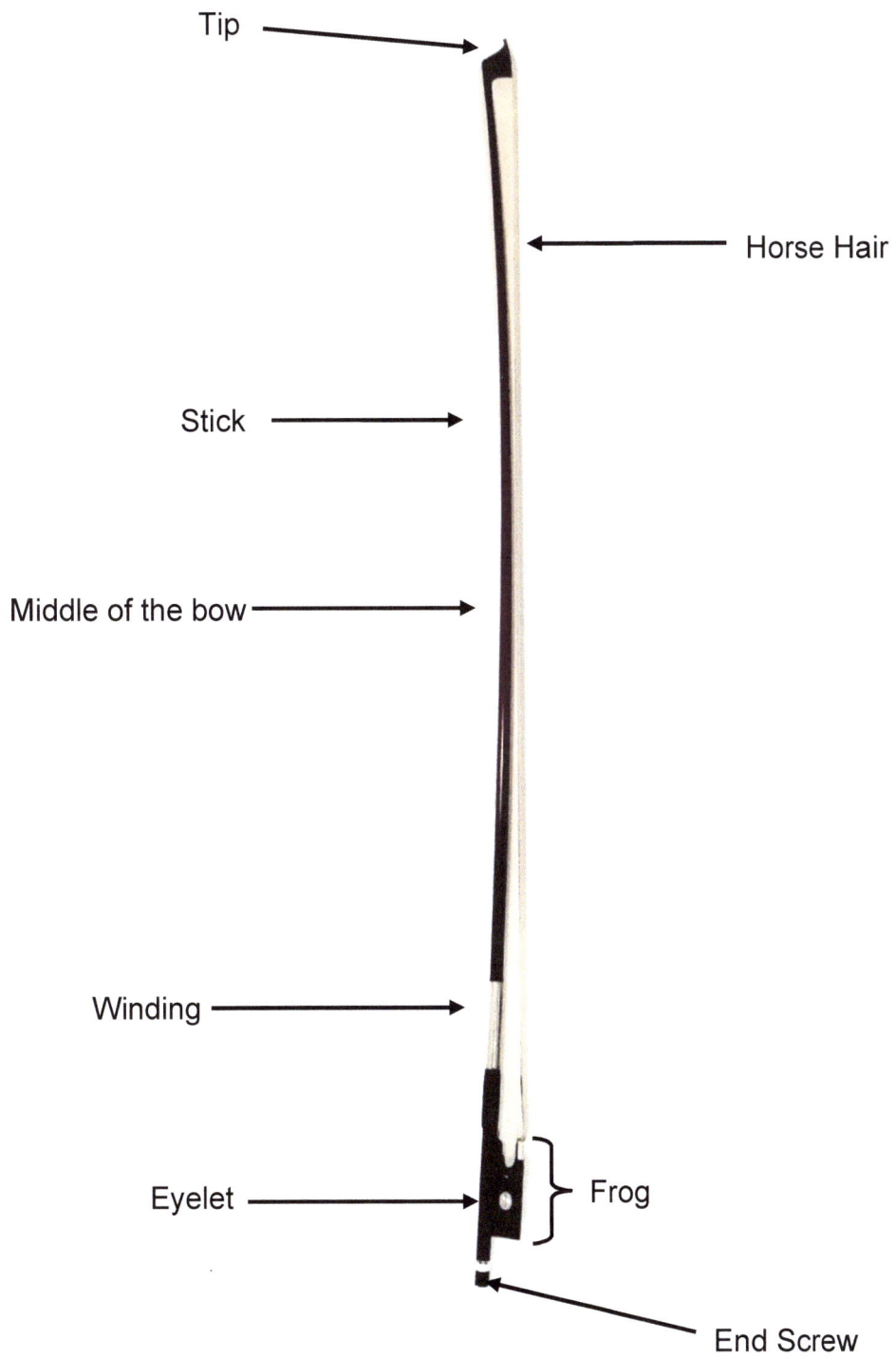

An Introduction to Music Theory

Pitches

C	D	E	F	G	A	B
Do	Re	Mi	Fa	Sol	La	Si

The Music Staff

The music staff (the pentagram) is used to notate music. It has 5 lines and 4 spaces. Each one of the lines and spaces represents a pitch. The name is given to each line and space depending on the clef.

The Staff

The Clefs

Music for viola is written in alto clef and sometimes in treble clef. The clef indicates the position of the notes in the music staff and gives each line and space a particular name. We can find the clef at the beginning of the music staff.

The Alto Clef (C-clef)

The alto clef for the viola is centered in the middle of the music staff (the third line). Because the c-clef is on this line, the line will be named C. When a note is on this line, it will have the same name as the line, which is C.

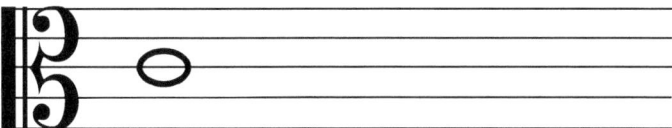

The Treble Clef (G-clef)

The treble clef for the viola is placed in the second line (going up) of the music staff. Because the circle of the g-clef is on this line, the line will be named G. When a note is on this line, it will have the same name as the line, which is G. The g-clef is used to read higher pitches, so we don't have to deal with many additional lines (ledger lines). For this method, we will not use the g-clef.

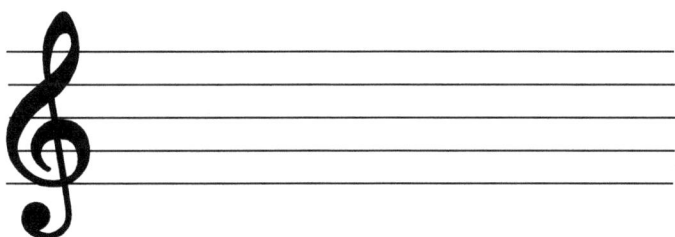

Names of the Spaces and the Lines of the Music Staff

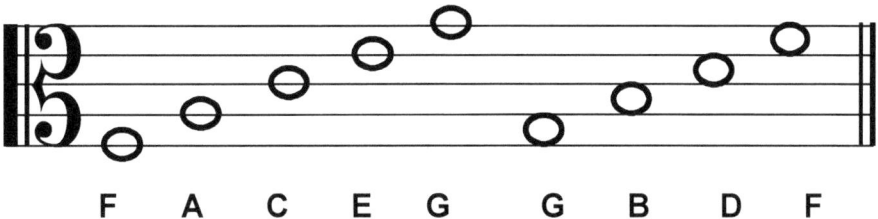

F   A   C   E   G   G   B   D   F

For all the exercises presented in this book, we are going to be using four notes only: C, G, D, and A, which correspond to the open strings of the viola.

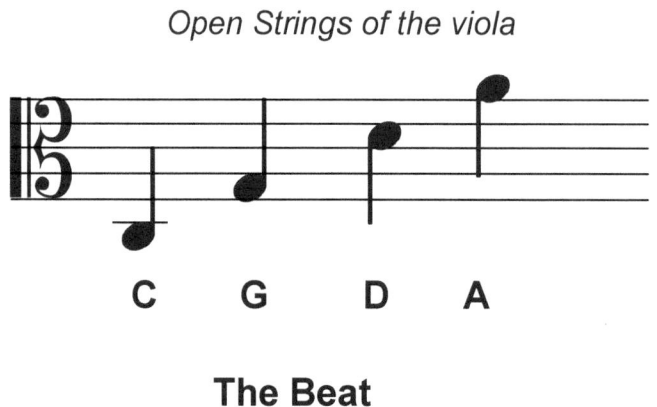

Open Strings of the viola

C   G   D   A

The Beat

The beat is the basic unit of time.

Note Duration

Musical notation indicates the duration of a sound. When we know the duration of a note, we will be able to perform music with precision. Also, depending on location of the note on the music staff, pitch will be different.

In this method, we will be using the following note value:

Symbol	Name	Value
𝗼	whole note	4 beats
𝅗𝅥	half note	2 beats
♩	quarter note	1 beat
♪	eighth note	1/2 beat
♬	sixteenth note	1/4 beat

Parts of the Note

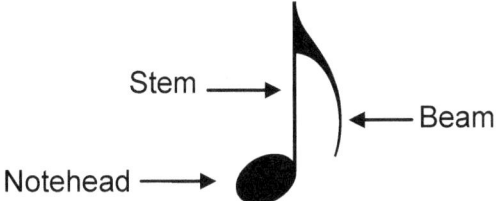

Rests

In order to make music we need silence; silence is important so we can hear and organize rhythm. When we place notes and rests together we can make different types of rhythms. We will be using in this method the following rests:

Symbol	Name	Value
𝄻	whole rest	4 beats
𝄼	half rest	2 beats
𝄽	quarter rest	1 beat
𝄾	eighth rest	1/2 beat
𝄿	sixteenth rest	1/4 beat

Time Signatures

The time signature tells us how many beats are in one measure (the top number) and what type of note represents one beat in the measure (the bottom number). We can find the time signature at the beginning of a piece, and in our case it will be at the beginning of each exercise. We are going to use only the simplest time signatures, seen below:

$$\frac{2}{4} \quad \frac{3}{4} \quad \frac{4}{4}$$

The Repeat Bar

The repeat bar tells us that we need to repeat a specific music passage.

Dynamics

Dynamics tell us how loud or soft the music should be played. We will use the following symbols:

Symbol	Name	Meaning
F	Forte	Loud
p	Piano	Soft
<	Crescendo	Gradually increasing volume
>	Decrescendo or diminuendo	Gradually decreasing volume

Rhythm

Rhythm is the placement of sound in time; we use accents, meters, and tempos as elements to organize sound and silence.

Bow Direction

We will use the symbols in this table to indicate bow direction.

Symbol	Name	Meaning
⊓	down bow	bow travels in the direction of the floor
V	up bow	bow travels in the direction of the ceiling

EXERCISES FOR CHILDREN

Knowing our Friend the Bow

These exercises will help you to remember how to hold the bow by memorizing the picture in each exercise. The exercises are designed to aid you while you are learning how to hold the bow. The use of illustrations will help you to understand the basics of holding the viola bow.

Holding the Bow

In this exercise each finger will have a name to help you understand where each finger has to be on the bow. Memorize each finger's name so you will remember it while practicing.

Directions

- Step 1: Ring finger goes on top of the moon (eyelet).
- Step 2: Middle finger goes right next to ring finger (because they are best friends).
- Step 3: Pointer finger goes on top of the pad (black material), placing the last joint of the finger on the bow.
- Step 4: Pinkie finger goes on top of the stick, **not** at the screw. This is very important. A good pinkie placement will form an arch; make a rainbow arch with the pinkie!
- Step 5: Your teacher will decide whether to place the thumb at the bottom of the frog or at the intersection of the stick and the frog. Regardless of the placement, begin by making

- a telescope shape with your right hand. Look at the shape of your thumb and make sure you keep this shape while holding the viola bow.
- *Words to remember*: moon, best friend, rainbow arch, pointer, telescope.

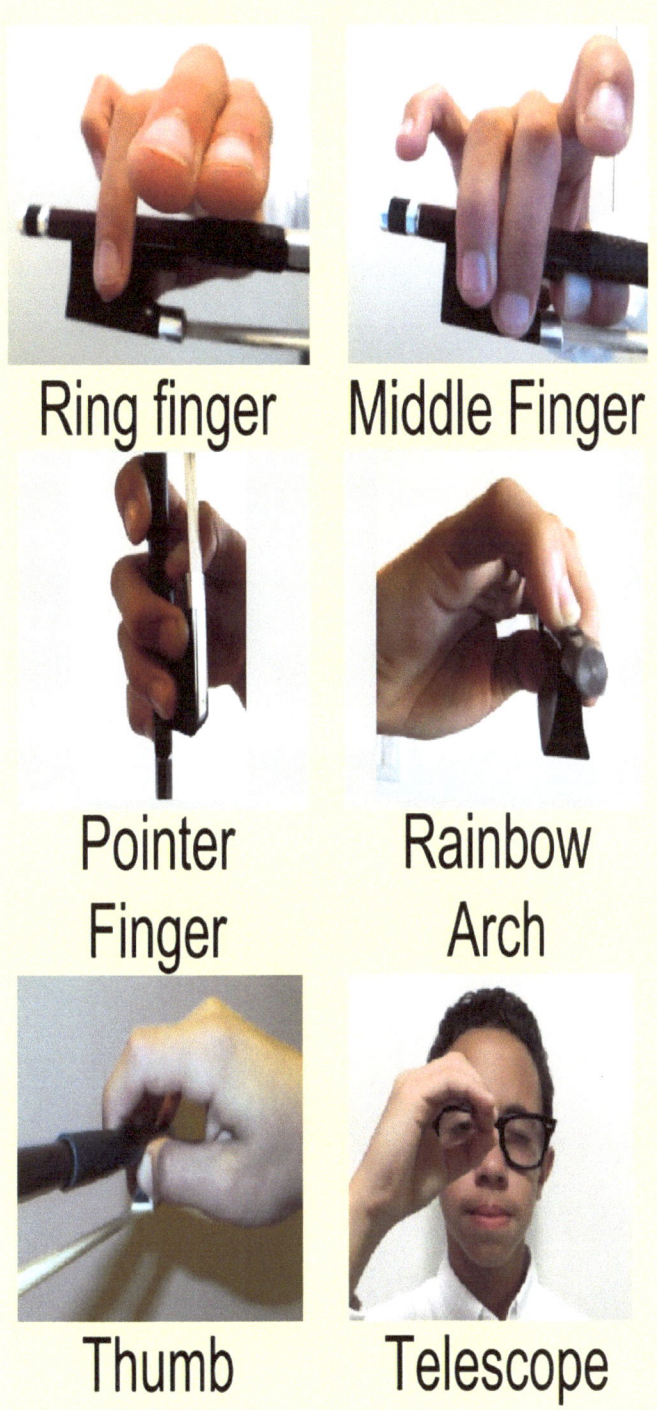

Ring finger   Middle Finger

Pointer Finger   Rainbow Arch

Thumb   Telescope

The Spider

Like a relaxed spider waiting for lunch, our fingers on the bow must be relaxed. Try to relax your hand and fingers when holding the bow to make a nice spider. Bend your fingers and crouch your hand down like a spider resting in his web. This will help you to create gorgeous sound and beautiful music.

Keep in Mind:

o Knuckles must remain hidden while holding the bow.
o Be relaxed.
o The back of the hand should be flat.

Word to remember: spider

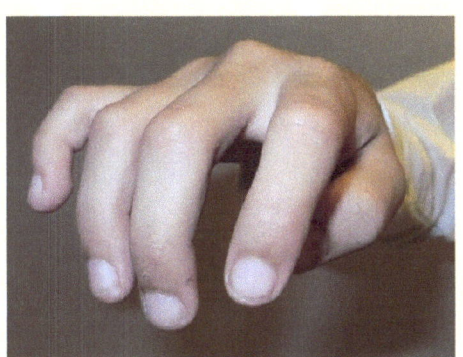

The Spider

Try to relax your hand and fingers!

The Rocket-Bow

Now that we know how to hold the bow, we will take off in our rocket-bow game. First, you need to hold the bow correctly, and then extend your bow-arm straight in front of you. Your bow is a rocket–bow! With the help of your teacher, move your arm (rocket-bow) towards the ceiling and make the take-off sound while you fly into the sky. The rocket-bow must remain straight at all times.

Your bow is a rocket bow!

Second, as soon as the rocket-bow gets to the sky, it is time to come down. Move your bow down (straight bow always) to the ground, making the landing sound until you get back to take-off position, and repeat.

This exercise will help to build elasticity in the wrist. Notice that the shape produced with the wrist when the rocket bow gets to the ceiling is the same shape that's made when the bow is at the frog. Also, the wrist shape as the rocket-bow is landing is the same when the bow is at the tip.

Word to remember: rocket-bow

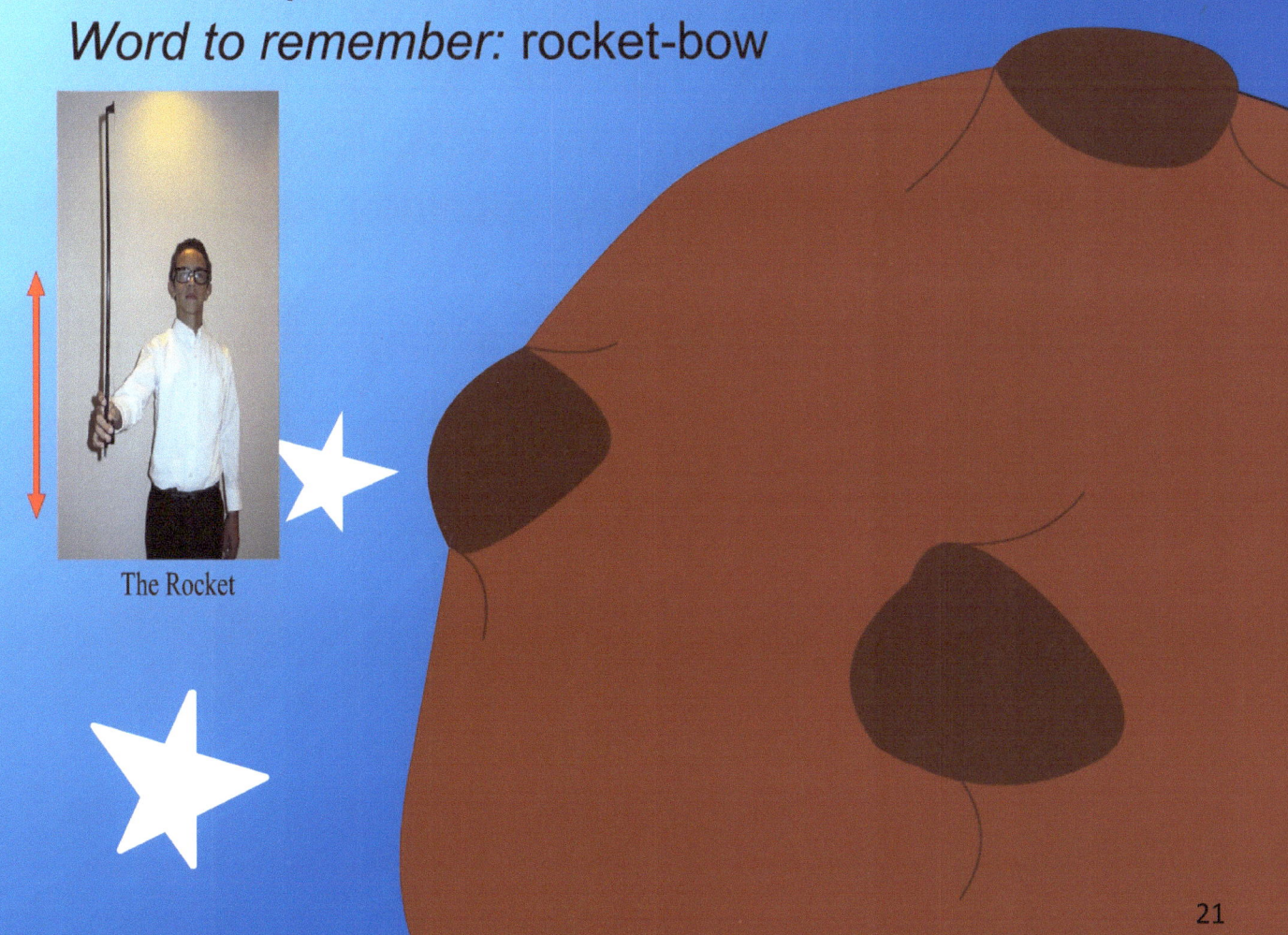

The Rocket

The Clock

The purpose of this exercise is to develop the hold of the bow and to understand how to manage the balance and weight of the bow.

This exercise is done in one of three ways. In the first approach, face the wall and hold the bow with a straight arm, touching the wall with the fingers the whole time. The bow will be the hour hand in this exercise, and the tip will touch each number. We will work with 12, 3, and 9 only. When the bow points to 12 o'clock, the focus is on holding the bow correctly and the weight of the bow is distributed evenly across all fingers. At 3 o'clock, although the bow is still held by all fingers, more weight is borne by the index finger. At 9 o'clock, more weight is borne by the pinkie.

This exercise must be done from 12 to 3, 3 to 12, 12 to 9, 9 to 12, 3 to 9 and so on. Make all combinations possible with the three hours, and at different speeds. This will develop balance and control.

The second approach is the same exercise, but without using the support of the wall. Try to keep the bow in a straight line all time.

The third approach is done only when you have learned how to hold the viola. In this exercise, begin with the bow at 12 o'clock, with the tip pointing at the ceiling as in clock exercise number 2. Then, while also holding the viola, bring the bow down to 9 o'clock; 9 O'clock will be any string on the viola. Start with the G-string and D-string. This exercise will teach you proper movement of the wrist, and will develop proper balancing of the bow when the entire bow's weight is on the pinky. *Word to remember:* clock.

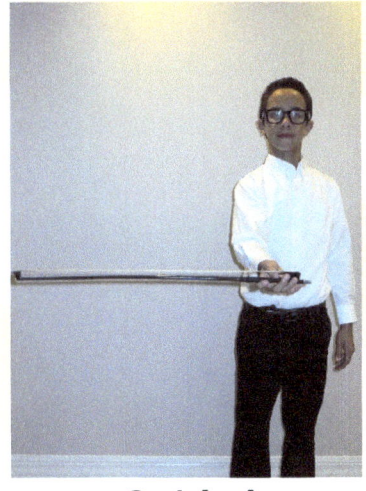
3 o'clock

12 o'clock

9 o'clock

The Rotunda

Before beginning this exercise, make sure your bow hold is correct. When it is, we will take a trip around the rotunda.

Stand with the left shoulder facing the wall. Extend the bow arm fully and point the tip of the bow at the center of the rotunda poster. The tip of the bow is your car. Begin at 9 o'clock and follow the arrows all around the rotunda. Your teacher will "direct the traffic" in the lesson.

This exercise will develop proper motion in the bow arm, control of the bow, and optimal bow hold. A sample poster will be included for this exercise.

Word to remember: Rotunda.

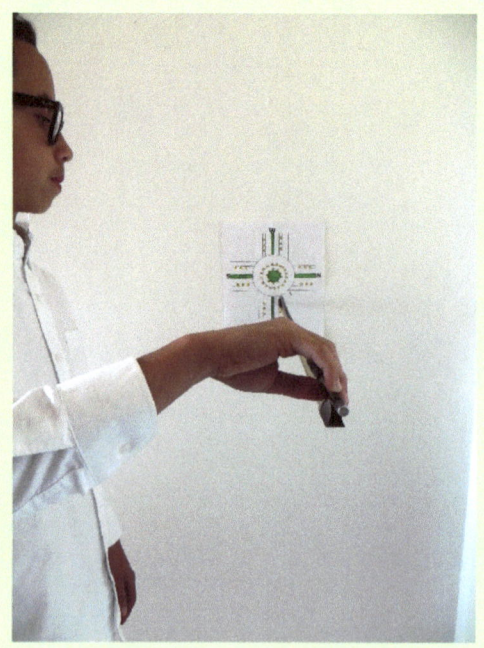

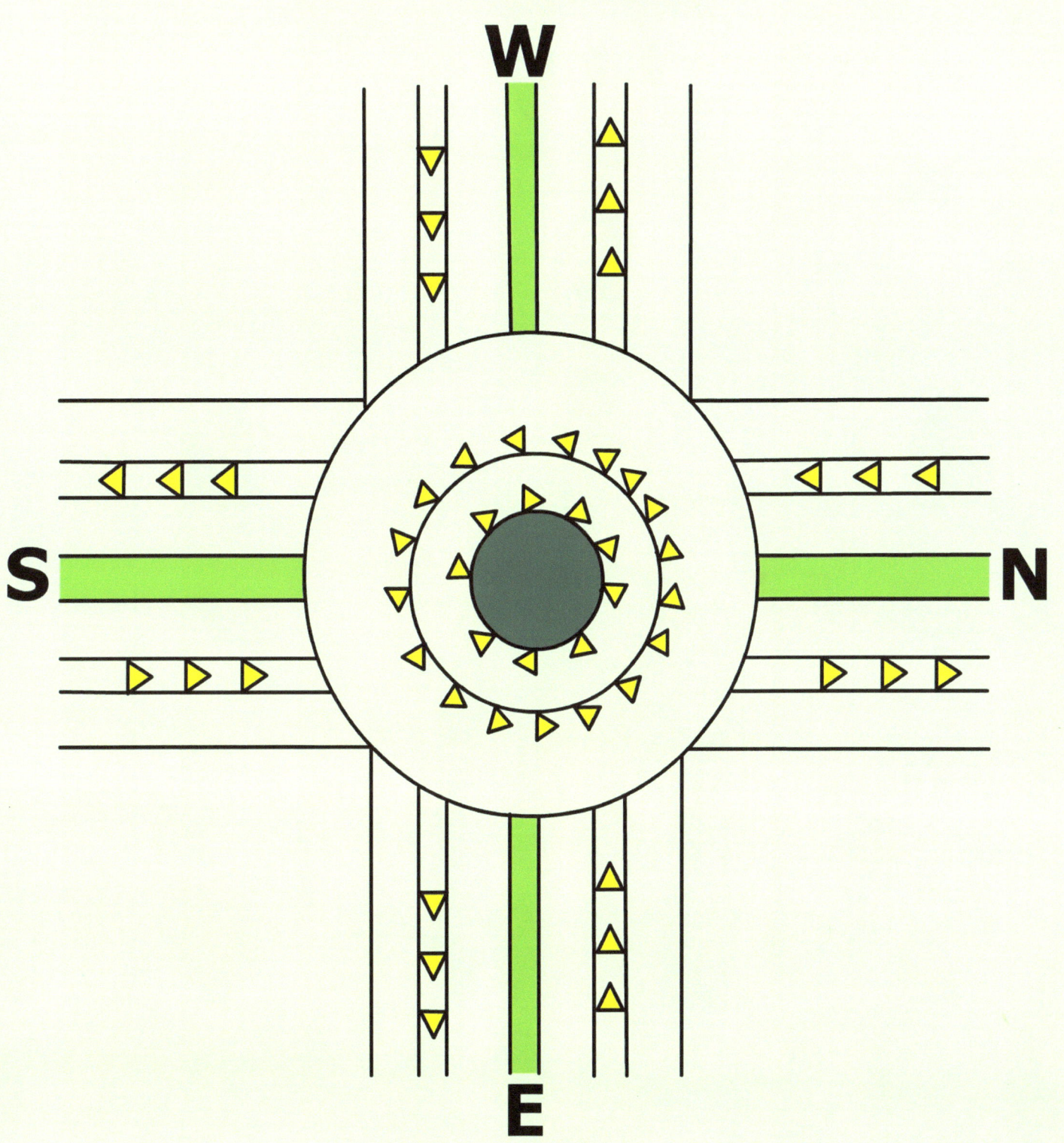

The Bow Knight

The purpose of this exercise is to help you develop good standing posture while playing the viola.

You are now The Bow Knight who stands up proudly with a straight back. A fine knight stance is also important. Make "V" for viola with your feet, and then open them to find balance. Remember to stand correctly and hold your viola and bow with pride because you are the Bow Knight.

Next, the Bow Knight will work with shapes on the bow-arm. Begin making the shapes just with the arm. Then practice with the bow, and finally, practice all shapes with the bow and viola.

Triangle (At the frog)   Square (At the midle of the bow)   Trapezoid (At the tip)

After learning the shapes, we will practice combinations between shapes. From triangle to square, from square to trapezoid, from trapezoid to triangle and so on.

Words to remember: knight and shapes

The Jump of Mr. Frog

My Friend, as always, before beginning this exercise, check to make sure your bow hold is correct. When it is, we are ready to help Mr. Frog jump from the frog to the tip of the bow.

Begin slowly. You should touch the string, with flat hair, at the frog section and   at the tip section. This exercise will help you to develop bow control, especially in terms of balance, weight control, distribution, and placement of the bow on the string.
"Word to remember: Mr. Frog."

Mr. Frog jumps back and forth!!!

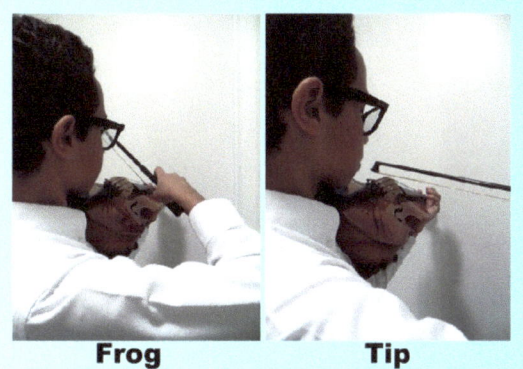

Frog   **Tip**

How to Do this Exercise:

- Mr. Frog goes from the frog to the tip (repeat).

- Mr. Frog goes from the tip to the frog (repeat).

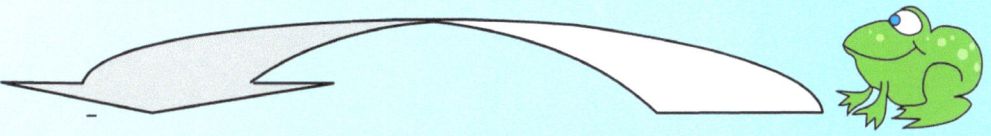

- Then, Mr. Frog jumps back and forth.

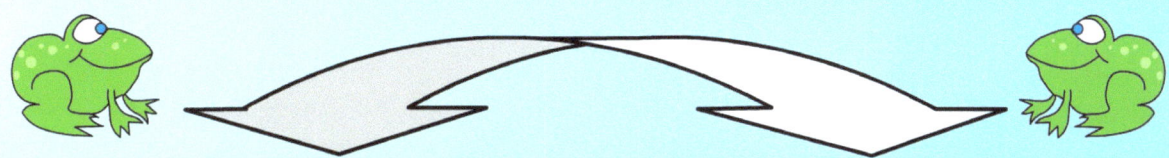

The Bow Train

Now we will start doing long notes on each string of the viola. In this exercise, we pay special attention to bow direction. The bow is going to be the Bow Train. The Bow Train will go from frog station to tip station and from tip station to frog station.

It is important to keep the Bow Train direction straight as it travels from one station to the other, so we can deliver our cargo safely while traveling on the railway-strings. The railway for this exercise will have a straight track, so our Bow Train will remain straight during all travel.

The hair of the bow will represent the wheels, so it has to be flat and keep contact at all time during the trip.

The cargo will be good sound, contact point, weight, and bow speed. Your teacher will decide how much bow, speed of bow, and weight will be applied.

First, do this exercise on one string, and then combine two strings. The bow goes up on one string, and then goes down on another. The Bow Train must make the trip on all the strings, and all train stations, frog station, middle station, and tip station.

Word to remember: the bow train

Frog Station   Middle Station   Tip Station

FROG STATION

My Bow Plane

In this exercise, the bow becomes an airplane. You must help the Bow Plane land smoothly on the runway. Again, first we need to check and correct the bow-hold, then prepare to land on the strings.

Beginner pilots should land their Bow Plane at the frog, while traveling down bow. Repeat until the landing is smooth.

You must help
The Bow plane, land smoothly
on the runway!!!

Then, practice the more difficult landing from the tip while traveling up bow.

It is important to land horizontally. Think about making a semi-circle with your hand while landing, in order to land properly. Do not land in a vertical line because the sound will be rough, like a crash.

This exercise will teach good attack, weight control, bow speed, and contact point control.
Word to remember: bow plane

Bow Arm Exercises (Open Strings)

Single String Exercises

Directions:
- Use whole bow (W.B).
- Always start on string.
- Contact point.
- Flat hair.
- Consistent bow speed.
- Practice this exercise at various tempos (largo, Adagio, Andante, Allegro, Presto).
- Practice using following crescendo and decrescendo patterns:

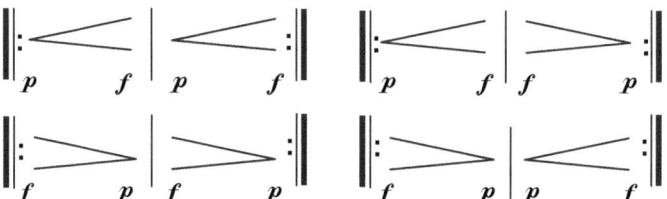

Exercise #1 (o : whole note)   R. Ramirez

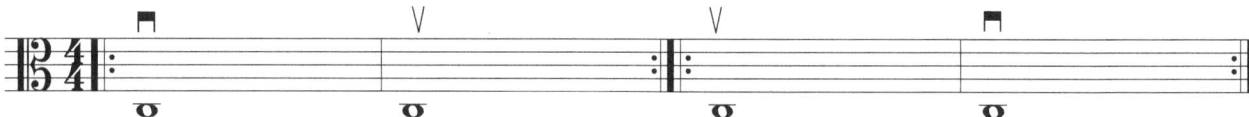

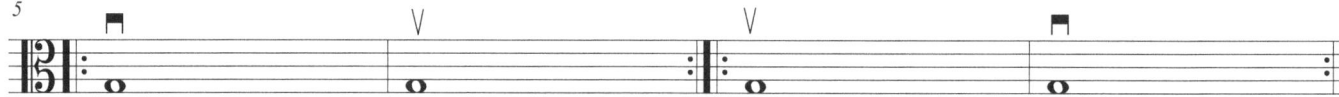

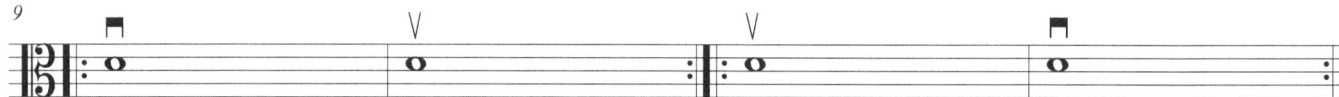

Connect all notes – Practice using the following dynamics: FF, F, mf, mp, p, pp

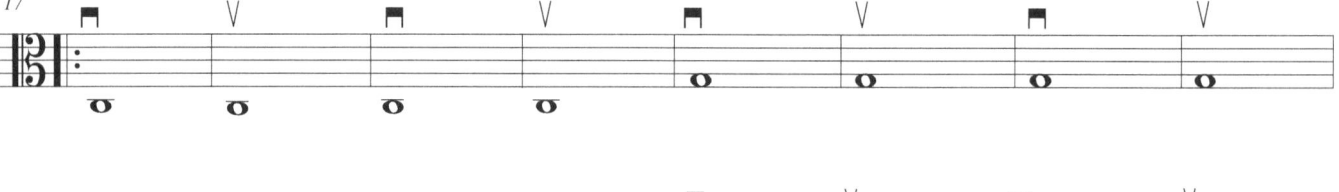

1.A. Whole notes, bow direction combination

Directions:

- To be performed with dynamics: F, p, FF, pp, mp, mf.
- Practice using the crescendo and decrescendo patterns from Exercise 1.
- Practice adding an accent > at the beginning of each note.
- Bow speed must remain the same whether V or Π throughout the whole note.
- Keep dynamics consistent for each note, connect each note to the other.
- Contact point, play with flat hair.
- Check fingers and posture.

R. Ramirez

1.B. Whole note and half note combination (To be practice on each string C,G,D,A)

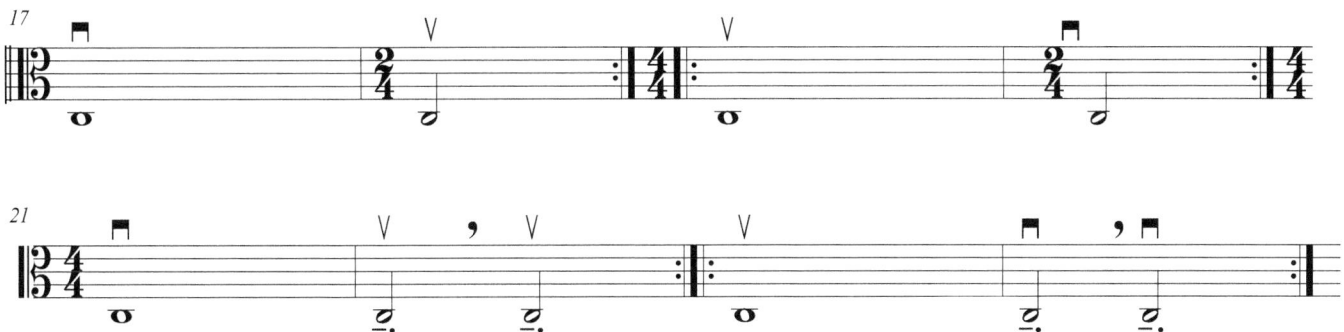

Exercise #2. ♩: The half note

Directions
- To be performed with dynamics: F, p, FF, pp, mp, mf.
- Practice using the crescendo and decrescendo patterns from Exercise 1.
- Practice adding an accent > at the beginning of each note.
- Bow speed must remain the same whether V or ⊓ throughout the whole note.
- Keep dynamics consistent for each note, connect each note to the other.
- Contact point, play with flat hair.
- Check fingers on the bow and general posture.
- Practice this exercise at various tempos.

Practice playing Ex. 2 from:
- Frog to middle bow.
- Middle bow to tip.
- On the middle of the bow.

Connect all notes

36

Exercise 2A. Half note Bow Direction Combination.

Directions:
- Practice on each string C, G, D, A.
- When two or more notes are to be played in succession with same.
bow direction (such as ⊓ ⊓ or V V V). Retake the bow; also can be detaché ⊓' ⊓' ⊓' etc.

Practice playing from:
- Frog to middle bow.
- Middle bow to tip.
- On the middle of the bow.

R. Ramirez

Exercise #3 ♩ : the quarter note

R. Ramirez

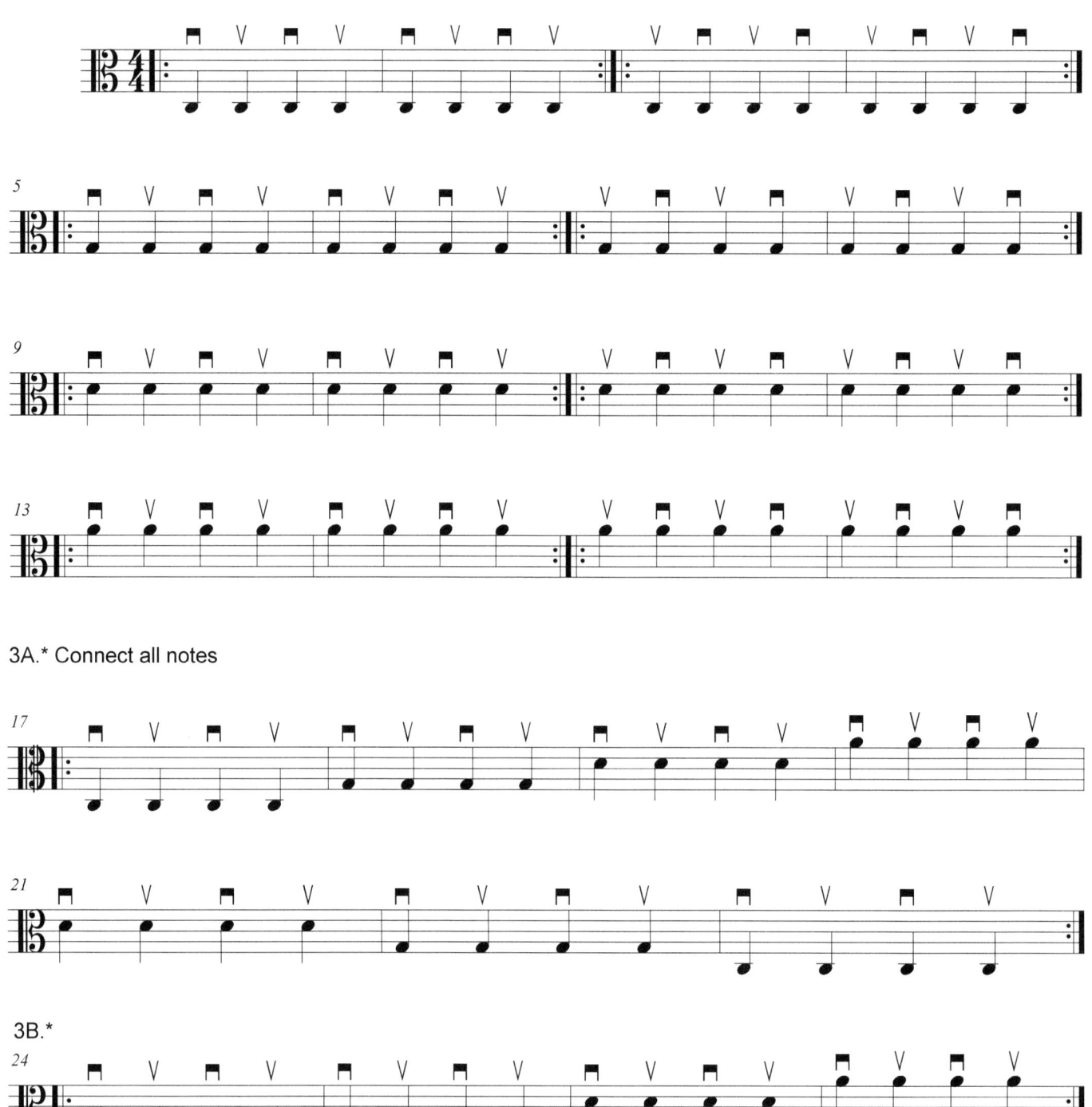

3A.* Connect all notes

3B.*

*Exercises 3A and 3B are also to be practiced using only ⊓ and V

Exercise 3C. The Quarter Note - Bow Changes

(To be practiced on each string C, G, D, A)

Directions:

Ex. 3C to be practiced using:
- Middle of bow, at the frog, at the tip, whole bow
- On the string at all times
- Legato stroke, detache stroke
- Start on the string

R. Ramirez

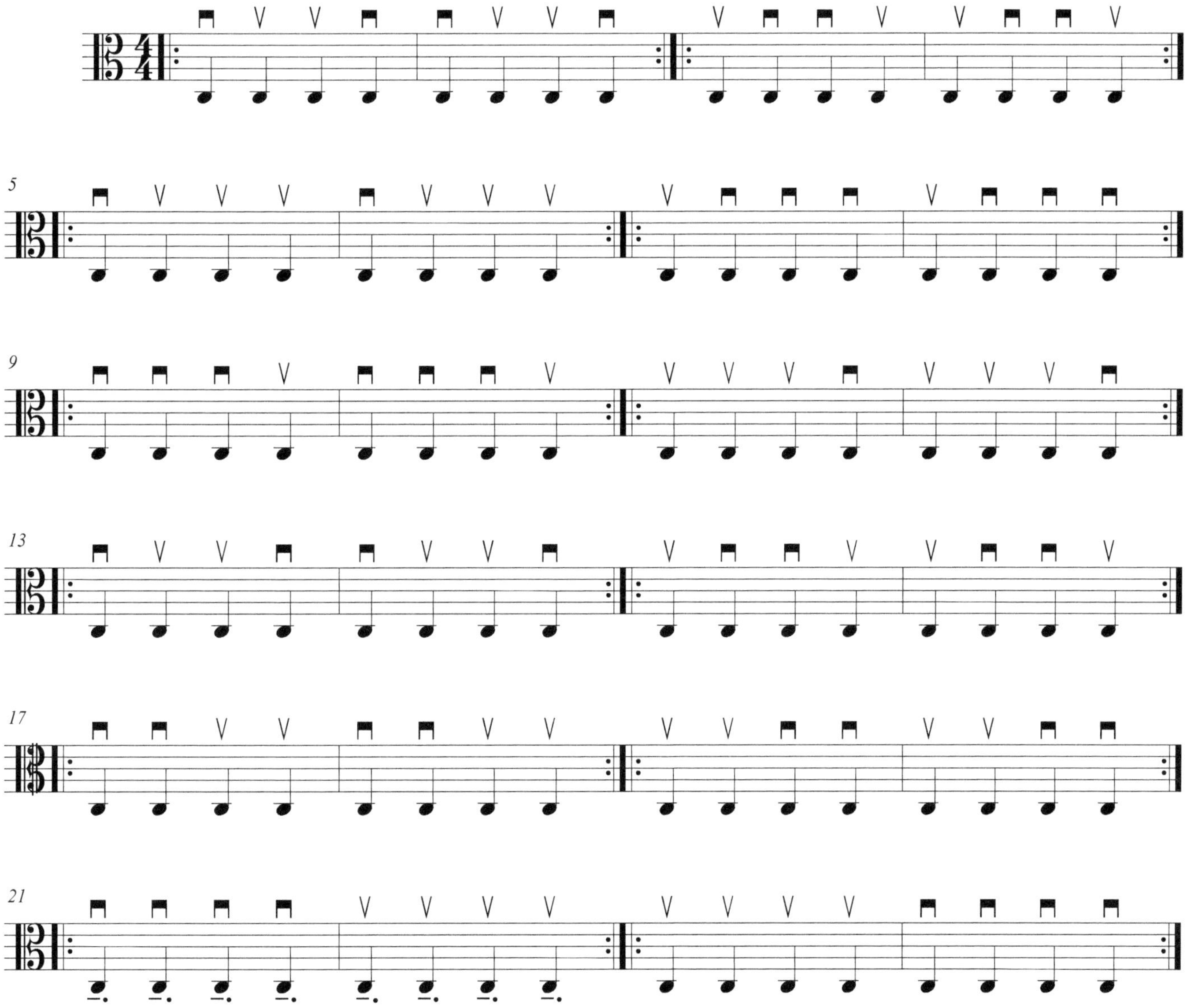

Also practice Exercise 3C using the following accent patterns:

Exercise 3D. The Quarter Note & Quarter Rest

(To be practiced on each string C, G, D, A)

Directions:
- Practice using various dynamic levels
- Start on the string
- Contact point
- Flat hair
- Maintain Same bow speed for each note group
- Begin slowly and gradually work towards a faster tempo

R. Ramirez

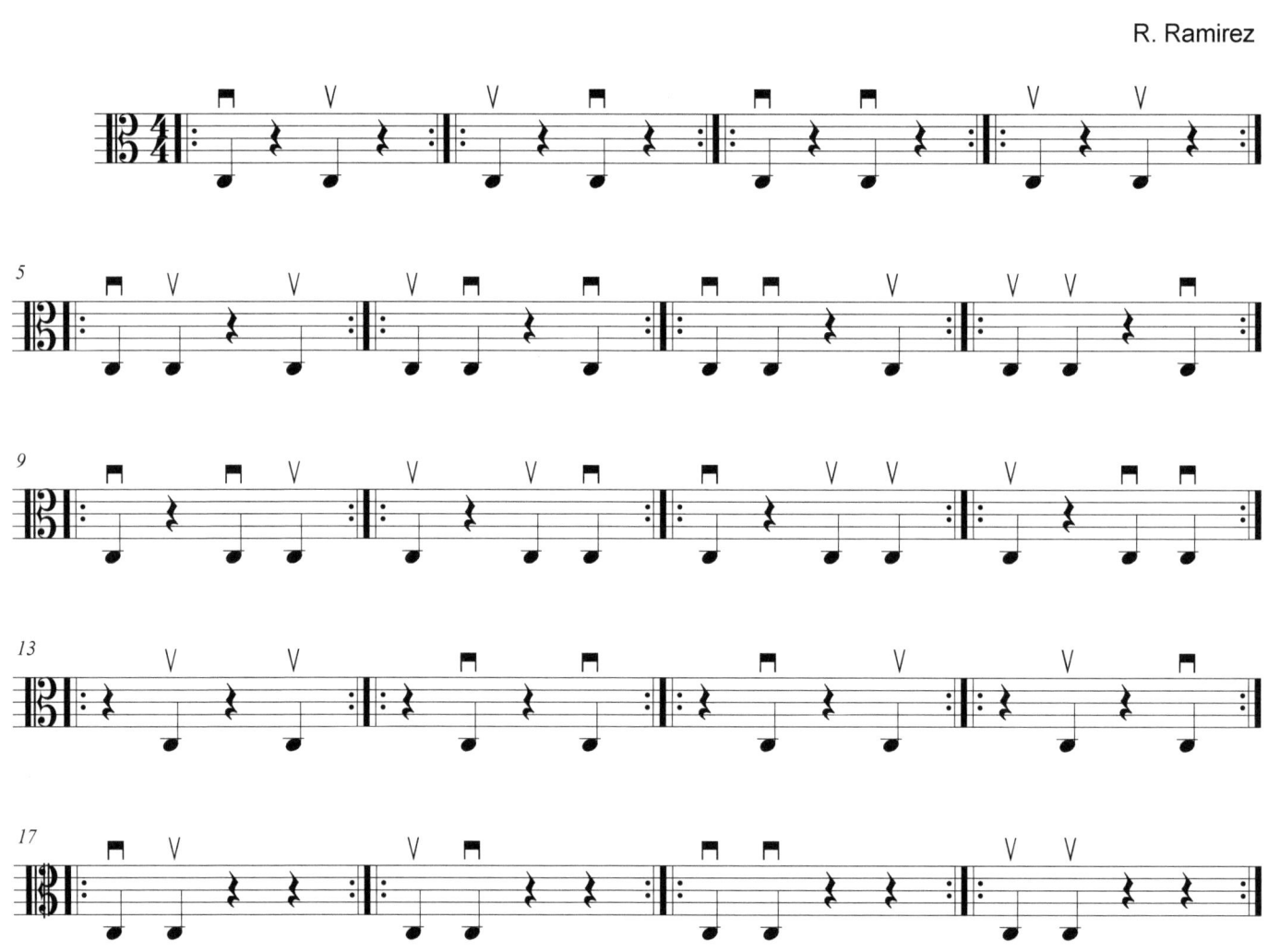

Exercise 4. ♪ The Eighth Note

(To be practiced on each string C, G, D, A)

R. Ramirez

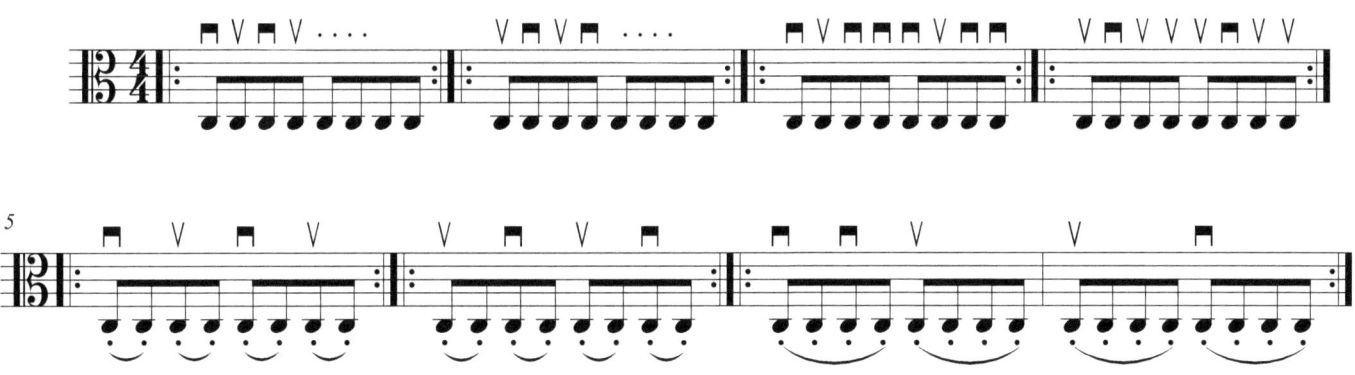

Exercise 5. The eighth note and eighth rest

Exercise 6. ♩ & ♪ Combinations

Directions:
- Use whole bow (W.B.).
- Always start on string.
- Contact point.
- Flat hair.
- Consistent bow speed.
- Practice this exercise at various tempo (Largo, Adagio, Andante, Allegro, Presto).
- Practice using following crescendo and decrescendo patterns:

R. Ramirez

42

Exercise 7. Quarter note & eighth note triplet combinations

R. Ramirez

43

Exercise 8. Quarter and sixteenth note combinations

R. Ramirez

8A.

8B. 8C.

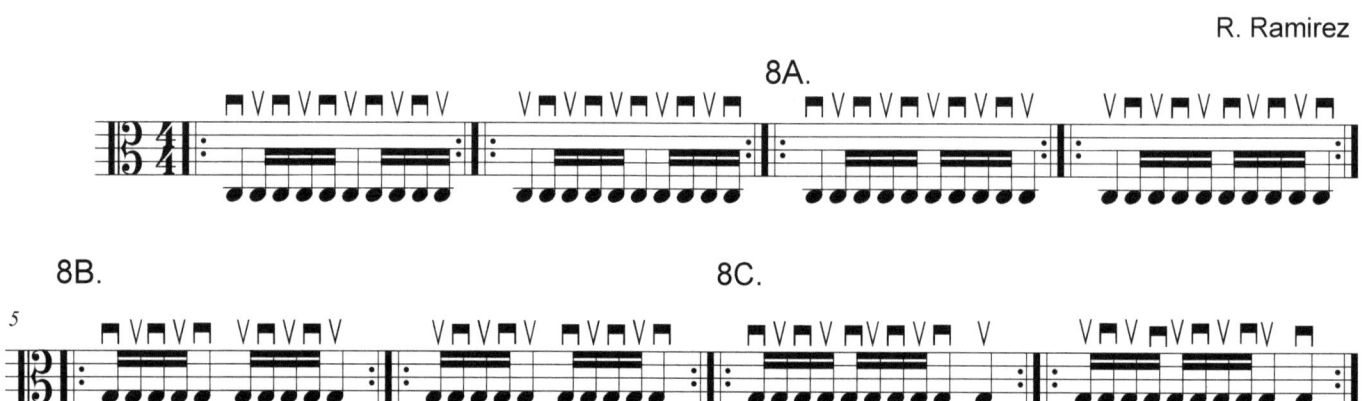

Exercise 9. Eighth, sixteenth, and quarter note combinations

9A.

9B. 9C.

9D. 9E.

9F. 9G.

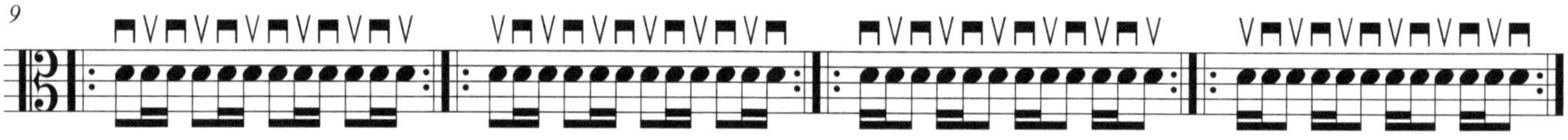

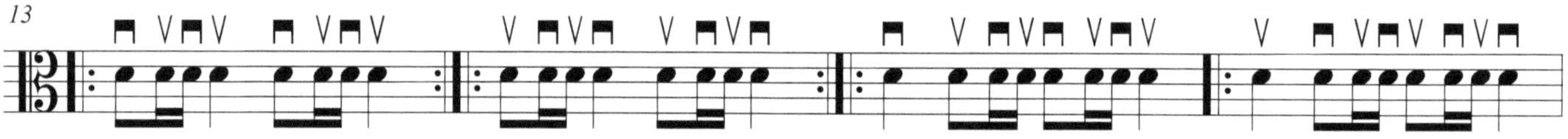

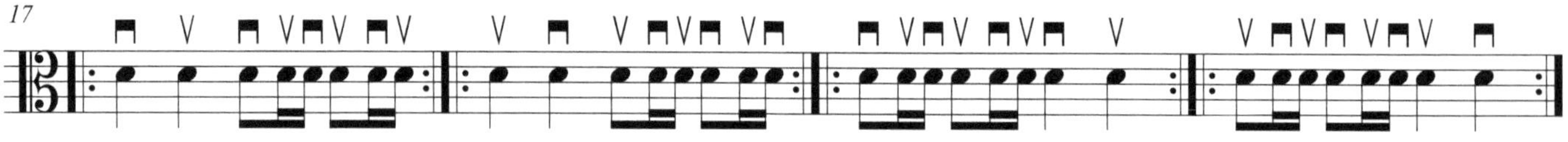

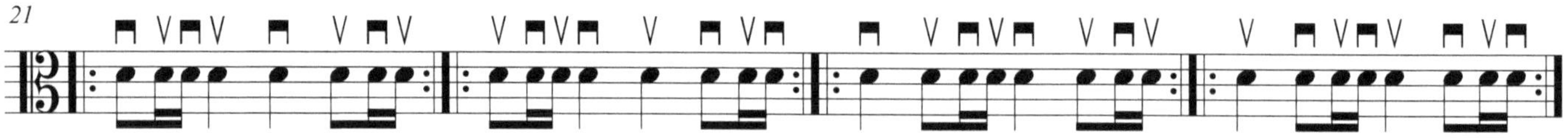

Exercise 10. Half, quarter, and eighth note combinations

R. Ramirez

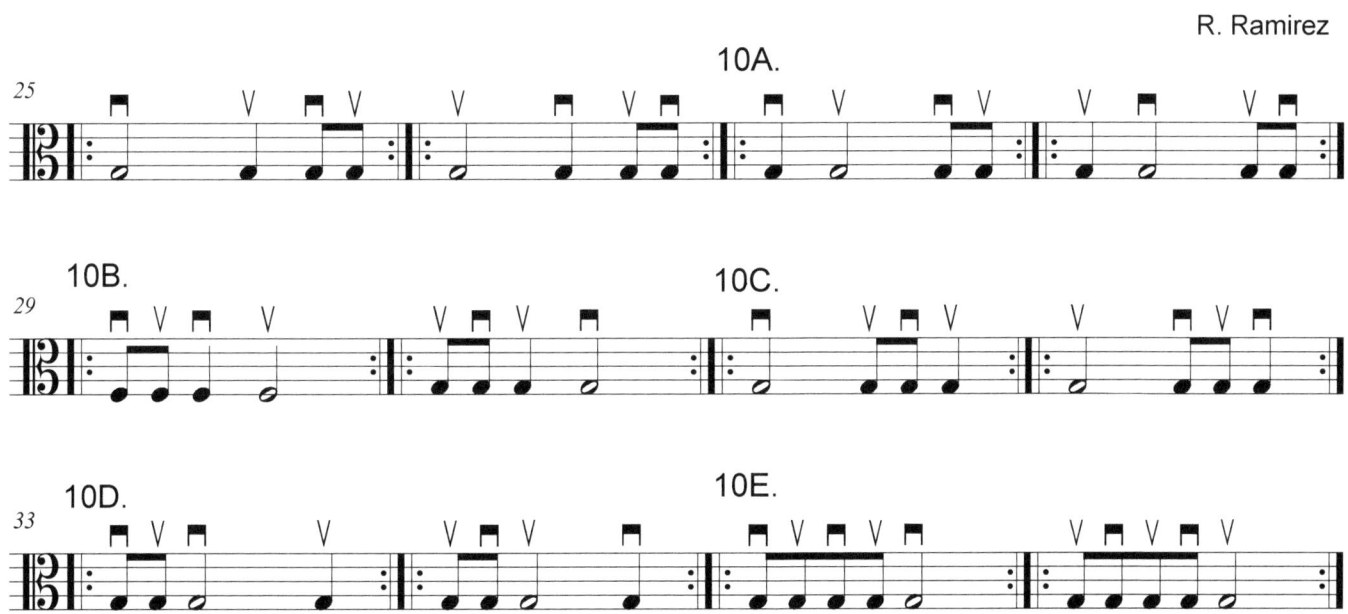

Exercise 11. Half note, quarter note, eighth note, and eighth note triplet combination

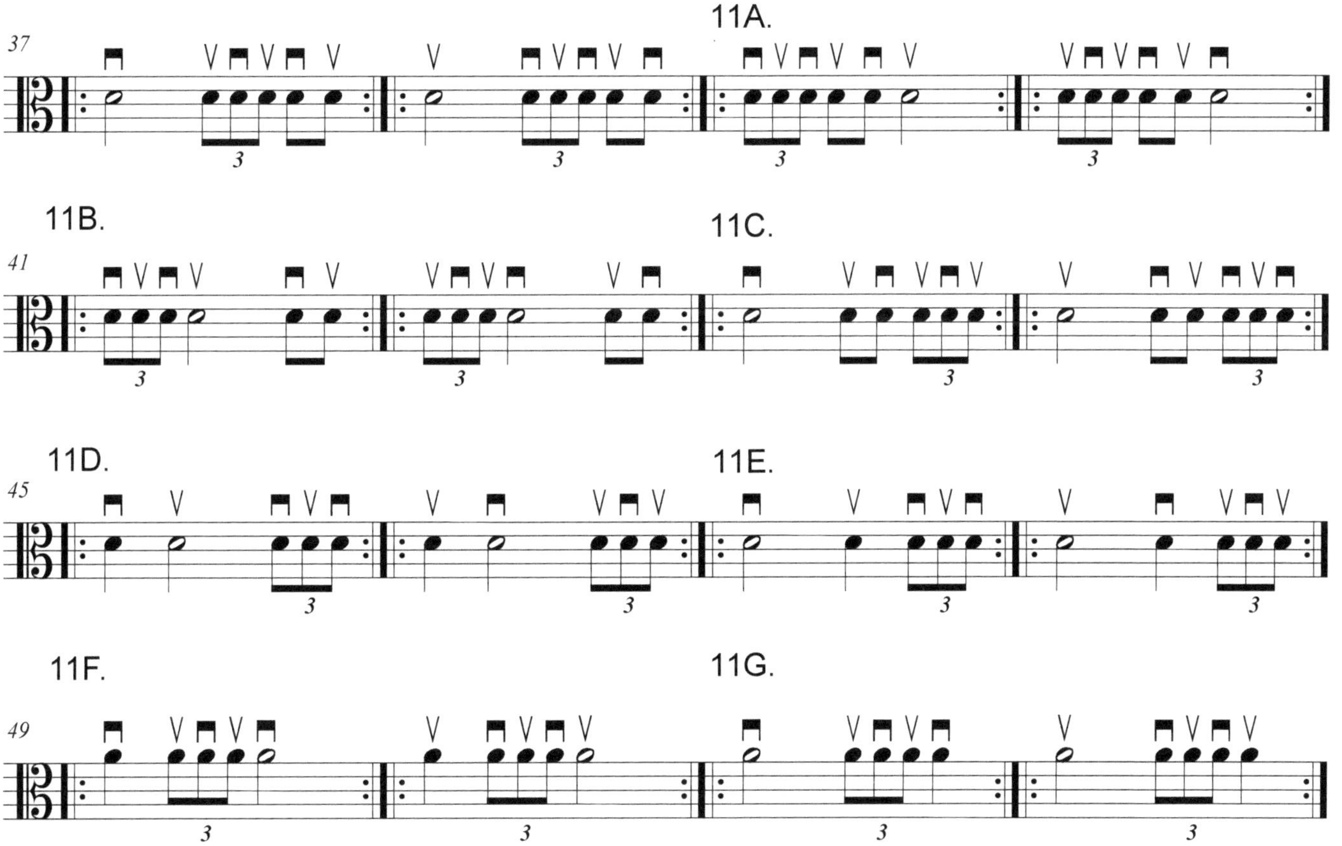

Exercise 12. Eighth, sixteenth, quarter, and half note combinations

R. Ramirez

Exercise 13. Dotted note combinations

R. Ramirez

Two String Crossing Exercises

Directions:
- Practice on all strings (2 at a time) C-G, G-D, D-A.
- Play on the string.
- Connected bow.
- Legato.
- Use varying dynamics (F, p, FF, pp), and with crescendo and decrescendo patterns.

R. Ramirez

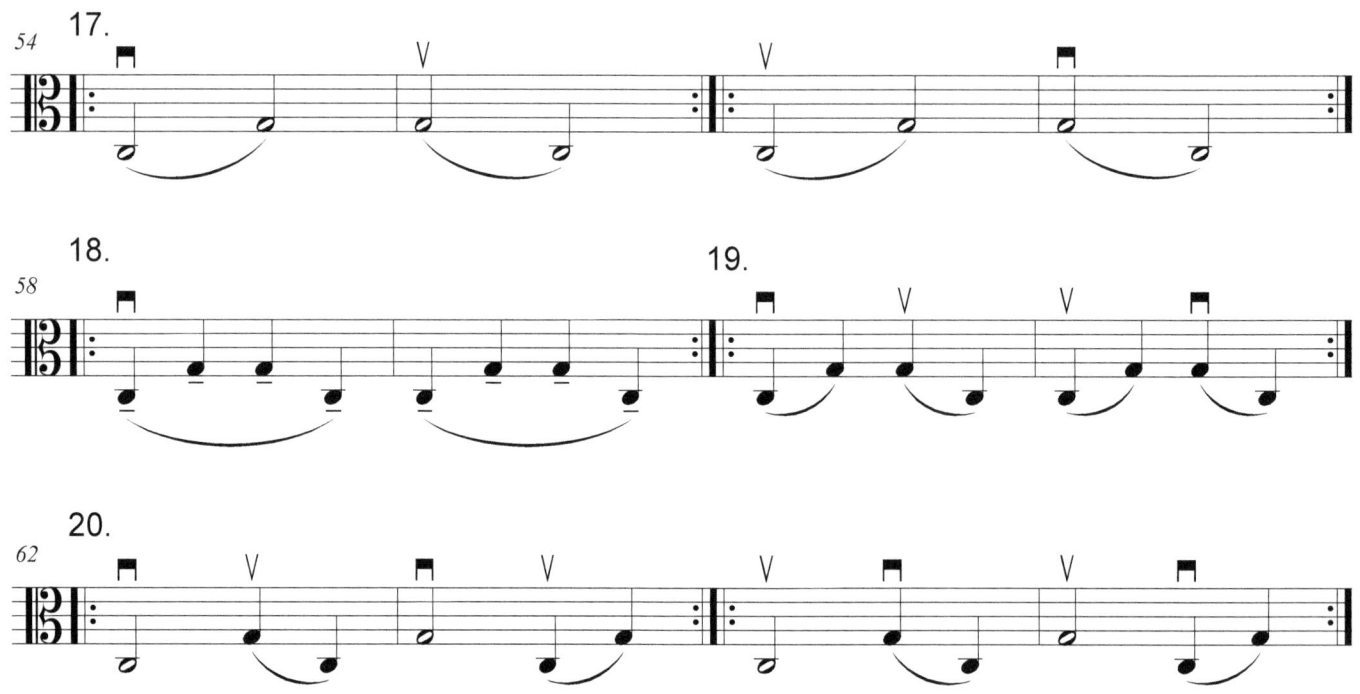

"The Wave" Exercise

Directions:
- To be practiced with, 𝅝, 𝅗𝅥, ♩ & ♪
- Practice only two strings at a time (C-G, G-D, D-A)
- Practice using various dynamic levels

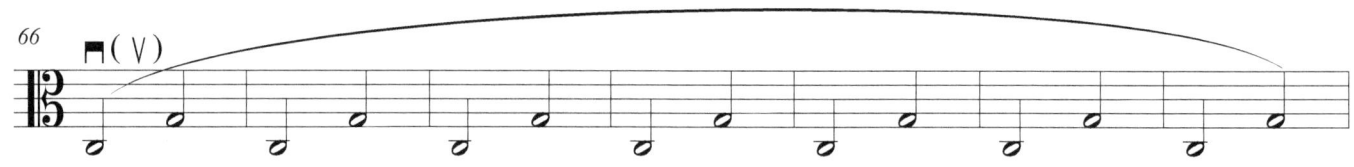